COACHES AND C

HOW TO WRITE A BOOK FOR YOUR BUSINESS IN 10 WEEKS OR EVEN LESS

'The surprisingly simple system to share your hard won knowledge with a wider audience than ever before – and get rightfully rewarded for the difference you make in the world'

✓ Attracts Clients
✓ Increases Your Reputation
✓ Makes More Money

Peter Thomson
'The UK's Most Prolific Information Product Creator'

Publishing in the United Kingdom by:
IngramSpark

Cartoons created by: Stephanie Smith, Leamington Spa Book design & layout by Velin@Perseus-Design.com ISBN Number: 978-1-3999-2366-8

(Paperback)

My sincere thanks to The Peter Thomson Team for all their continued love and support.

Why write a book?

As you and I are involved in the helping industry of coaching, consulting, speaking, training, or therapy, why would we want to write a book?

We need to have that 'why' firmly in our mind.

There are number of reasons why...

1. We want to improve the impact we have in the market, don't we?

2. We want to reach more people than we could dream of reaching on just a one-to-one basis. That way we can have a greater influence.

3. We can get our knowledge, our experience, our expertise, and what I call the 'magic ingredient' out there – and change people's lives.

By the way, that's where the money is...

In the magic ingredient.

I'll come back to that for you later in the book.

- We can get impact.
- We can get influence, and

- We can get income, and
- We can enjoy significance.
- By so doing we build a business and a life of choice.

I don't know about you, but for me, 'choice' is what I want:

- I want to choose **how** I work.
- I want to choose **who** I work with.
- I want to choose **why** I work.
- I want to choose **my income levels**.
- I want to choose **my holiday levels**.
- I want to choose to **help other people**.

All of these ideas are based on that one philosophy …

"Money is Simply the Silent Applause for a Job Well Done"

So why am I qualified to share these ideas with you?

Well, to start with - I'm going to be sharing with you some of my cards from the deck of writing, creating, and marketing informational products.

Starting in business in 1972…

I built 3 successful companies – selling the last to a public company, after only 5 years trading, for £4.2million – enabling me to retire at age 42.

It's taken me 50 years in business so far to learn what I know and 30+ of those years helping coaches, consultants, speakers, and trainers, and fellow professionals to be more successful by showing them how to get paid the right fee; by showing them how to write, create, and market informational products to get their message out there, making a difference, and having fun in the process.

Now regarded as 'The UK's Most Prolific Information Product Creator' and Nightingale Conant's main UK author, over those 30+ years **I've spent over £400,000 learning great stuff**, going on seminars and buying books, audio and video training programmes.

At one stage...

In my collection from Nightingale-Conant alone, I had 267 audio programmes. I'm a lifelong audio junkie. I attend seminars, webinars, and all this stuff because I know this:

We must keep on learning good new stuff, mustn't we?

"The day we stop LeaRNING is the day we stop EaRNING!"

-Peter Thomson

So, let's get going...

To find out whether we really can take what we know and make money by sharing it with people. Can we make a difference to people's lives by sharing what we know with others? Yes, we can!

Table of Contents

~

Chapter 1 - Let's Get Focused

N ow, something important to start; the disclaimer.

- I don't know you yet.
- I don't know your business.
- I don't know your experience.
- I don't know your level of commitment.
- However, I believe you are committed because you're reading this.

And I know the ideas I'm going to share with you work, because I've used them myself. They work for me. I know they work for a number of my clients, because many of my clients have made 1,000,000… 500,000… 250,000… 100,000… 20,000… and nothing!

So, I can't guarantee any outcome for you.

All I can guarantee is that I will do my utmost, my very best, open my cupboard doors and tell you the stuff that's worked and the stuff that hasn't worked.

But it's over to you to put in the effort, the energy, the investment, the commitment to make this work, to get your message out there, change the world, and build for yourself a business and life of your choice.

"In the beginning you do a lot of stuff you don't get paid for, so that in the future you get paid for a lot of stuff you don't do"

-Peter Thomson

You and I have got to put the effort and the energy in first to create our product.

Question #1:

How much extra income do you want each year?

Question #1

1. How much extra income do you want each year?

Bank of Life

I want an extra   £ [   ]

per _____ because _____

_____

000150   23 2945   51179883 12   *Financial Freedom*

What's the 'why' that's driving your decision to have that extra income?

Get clarity on your 'why,' and I'll explain 'why' in a moment or two.

Question #2:

How much extra time do you want each year?

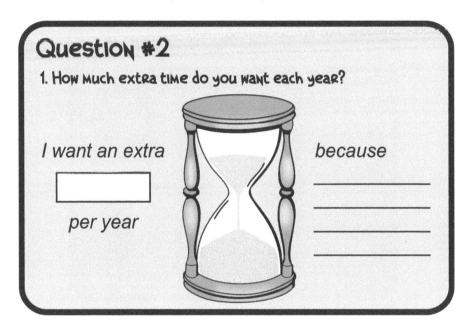

I reached a period in my life where I started taking an extra month off every year. I did that for six years running to the point where I had six months on and six months off.

And like Stephen Covey said,

"Put the big stones in the jar first"

In other words, you book your holidays first, because if you don't, you'll find that the sand, gravel and pebbles of life will have filled up your time and there's no room for holidays!

If you wait to book your holidays, you know as well as I do that life can take over and suddenly you find a year has gone by and you think to yourself, "What happened?"

Question #3

How serious are you?

10 out of 10 is obviously massively serious. 0 = not serious!

Now, here's a thought for you...

What will happen for you and other people if you don't share your knowledge or experience, your expertise, and your magic ingredient, with the world?

Well, lots of things happen.

They don't get to change their lives for the better, because what you and I do is: we either help someone solve a problem, or we help them capitalise on an opportunity. Isn't that true?

And if we don't do that...

- If we don't help people, there's no difference.

- If there's no difference, we don't get paid.

- And if we don't get paid, then we've got to do something else in our lives, whereas we're really, as far as I'm concerned, in the best business in the world.

So, what we're going to cover is...

How to write and create and market YOUR information products.

Most people tell me they've got a bit of a problem of getting their knowledge out of their heads and onto paper.

Some people say, "Well Peter, which product do I make?"

I'm going to show you how to make several different products with the same material.

I've collected, over the last 25 years, a list of 92 ways to use the same information.

And then, of course, the most important thing is marketing, isn't it?

We're not in the business we're in; we're in the business of marketing the products and services of the business we're in. Makes some sense, doesn't it?

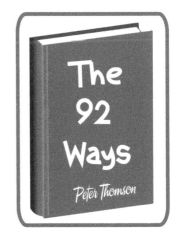

Everything we discuss is based on this idea…

"Resistance is created through a lack of clarity"

This comes from a brilliant book called 'Switch' by Chip and Dan Heath. What a fabulous expression!

- Which book shall I write?
- Shall I write a book?
- Should I turn it into an online or offline or whatever?

Resistance is created through lack of clarity on email marketing, on your website and direct mail, on speaking to a client. You must have (and create) clarity. Without clarity you and I can't move forward.

Without clarity your clients can't move forward. And we're talking about the difference between clients and customers. There's a big difference there.

This is what we're going to do...

"Create a Business and a Life of Choice!"

- When you become an author, you get more leads.
- Because you get more leads, you get more clients.
- Because you get more clients, you get more respect.
- Because you get more respect, you make more money.
- Because you make more money, you get more time.
- And because you've got more time, you can write more books.

I've written so many books, so many audio and video programmes.

In fact...

15 Books, 10 Booklets, over 100 audio programmes, 100 video programmes, and online stuff. I've written 1,000 e-zines that I've turned into books, and I'll show you how to do that as well.

We can leverage what we know. It's just so much fun to do it!

TO DOWNLOAD YOUR FREE COPY NOW - GO TO

**WWW.PETERTHOMSON.CLUB/
BOOK-WRITING-TEMPLATE**

Chapter 2 -
The 4 Critical Questions

We must answer these four critically important questions, before we get into any writing. Most people will think about questions #1 and #2, but most people don't think about questions #3 and #4.

Let's do them together now.

Question #1 – Who am I?

Now, what do I mean by that? *Who am I?*

You must decide before you start to write, before you write anything, before you write your book, before you write a webpage or an email, before you write anything, *who the heck are you*?

Are you somebody who has had some great **results** in life so therefore you are able to share how you achieved those results with people?

Or are you somebody who's done a lot of **research**—you've been online, and you've been offline, and you've investigated, and you have great information to share with somebody?

Or are you perhaps like Napoleon Hill? You are a **reporter**, and you've been out and interviewed successful people?

I've interviewed 174 successful people in all walks of life.

Many of the names you would know, because they're well known, like Jay Abraham, Robert Cialdini (the author of *'Influence Science and Practice'*), Brian Tracy, Jay Abraham… the great and the good, and a variety of other people from business, all sorts of different people… even the magician Paul Daniels and the co-originator of NLP, Dr Richard Bandler!

I've learned so much through those interviews, and of course, I can report on what they taught me – as well.

So, I'm fortunate I've have all three of those.

- I've had some great results in life, including in this industry for the last 30+ years.
- I've interviewed lots of people, I've done some reporting, and
- I've done loads of research, because I'm a regular attendee of webinars, seminars, and I read books all the time.

So, that's what you do, because remember this it's important

"You don't get paid for what you do,
You get paid for what you've done"

-Peter Thomson

Question #2 – Who are they?

Once you've got that clarity, remember our expression here.

"Resistance is created through a lack of clarity."

So, if you have clarity about who you're talking to, it's easier to talk to them—so much easier. And when I share with you the other 2 questions, it'll all become even clearer.

Question #3 - Who am I to them?

Let me explain who I am to my marketplace—to the coaches, consultants, speakers, and trainers I've been dealing with for 30+ years. This is going to sound somewhat unusual. I am 'Uncle Peter'.

Now, that's me naturally. 'Uncle Peter' is the person who expects you to be the best you can be.

He doesn't take any excuses. He'll take an odd reason, but he won't take any excuses. He will be totally and utterly and brutally honest with you.

He will explain what to do clearly, unambiguously, and expect you to do it, because he wants you to be more successful.

Now, that's who I am; that's my very nature. I'm a classic 'high D,' if you've done any DISC profiling. A classic 'A' shape… I want to get it done. I want to help you get it done.

So, who are you?

- Are you a trusted advisor?

- Are you their best friend and you put your arm around their shoulder?

- Are you somebody who stands on the side, waving the flag and cheering?

- Or are you out at the front - leading?

It makes a difference to how you communicate with your audience, so get clarity about who you are to them.

Question #4 - Who are they to me?

In other words, are they on one side of the scale, where they've never heard of you, so they don't know you and don't know if they like you? They don't know if they trust you. They've never bought before.

Or are they all the way over on the other side of the scale, where they know you, they like you, they trust you, they've bought from you before many times.

Because the way you communicate across this timeline is so different.

Not many people know this, and I've tested it, so I have proof that it's right.

On the first side of the scale, the message will more likely be 'Away Motivated'. But on the other side of the scale, it can be away or towards –particularly towards works well. We'll talk more about that as we go through.

"If a person empties their purse into their head, no one can take it away from them - an investment in knowledge always pays the best interest"

- Benjamin Franklin

Chapter 3 -
The 10 x 10 Formula -
Writing Your Book in 5 Days

~

First of all, decide on the overall topic, then answer the following questions:

Question #1 - What is the possible title?

The title of my book is:

_____

The strapline is:

_____

I'll use one of mine as an example.

The title is: **'The Secrets of Communication.'** And the strapline is **'Be Heard and Get Results.'**

Not a very great strapline, I have to say, but I did write this some years ago. The title of the book tells you what's the umbrella topic area you're talking about. My topic here is obviously communication.

- What's your title?
- What's the overall umbrella topic area?
- What's the strapline? (The words under the main title which add clarity about the benefits the reader will enjoy)

Write them in the box and then we'll go on to the next question. Remember – this is only your first stab at this. You don't have to get it right yet. You must get started.

Question #2 – What are the 10 or more chapters I want to include in my book?

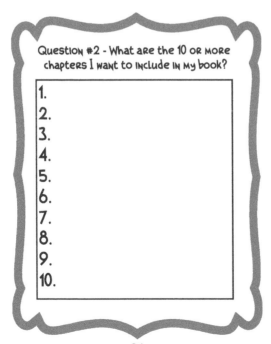

Question #2 - What are the 10 or more chapters I want to include in my book?

1.
2.
3.
4.
5.
6.
7.
8.
9.
10.

So, for example - 10 chapters, based on my book example, would be:

So for example - 10 chapters, based on my book example, would be:

1. The Power of Active Listening
2. The Subconscious Encoding Process
3. Reaching Home Base
4. The Eyes Have It
5. Questioning Skils
6. Starting a Conversation
7. Body Language - The Unspoken Truth
8. Open and Closed Questions
9. The LAnguage Itself
10. Factors and Incentives

Now, answer the question:

"What are the 10 or more tips I want to possibly include in the chapter on _____'

Now, it becomes a tip if it starts with a verb.

Let me give you some examples…

These are from one of my tips booklets *'117 Ways to Get Almost Anyone to Do Almost Anything'*, these are some of the verbs I've used to start a tip with:

Consider
Insert
Use
Practise
Show
Ask
Change

What I want you to do for the moment is **write down just about 10 tips for one of your chapters.**

TO DOWNLOAD YOUR FREE COPY NOW - GO TO
WWW.PETERTHOMSON.CLUB/
BOOK-WRITING-TEMPLATE

What I want you to do for the moment is write down just about 10 tips for one of your chapters.

My 10 possible tips are:

1.
2.
3.
4.
5.
6.
7.
8.
9.
10.

You now have some chapters

Now you've put tips in one of the chapters and you can go through and write even more tips for that chapter, and all the other chapters, later.

Congratulations … You're on the way!

And now I'll show you how it all comes together.

This is called…

"The Magic of Maths and the Fascination of Fractions"

-Peter Thomson

Let's imagine we have **10 chapters with 10 tips.**

If you write 10 chapters with **10 tips, that's 100 tips.**

Now, if you write **one paragraph per tip of about 20 words,** that'll be a total of **2,000 words** in your tips booklet, which is where we're starting the process.

Just so you know, this is the process I use to create all my informational products.

It's just so simple. When I show it to people on my open seminars they say, "What? Peter, is it this simple?" I say, "Yep, it's simple but it's not always easy, because it takes strength of character to actually do it, doesn't it?"

So, what does 20 words look like?

I'll give you an example...

"Remember when you're studying someone's face to look for the red triangle in the corner of the eye disappearing."

That's 20 words!

The little red triangle, by the way, is called the caruncle, which is in the corner of the eye, called the inner canthus.

Could you write 20 words for each of the 100 tips about a subject you know and are passionate about?

And the answer is, "Yes, Peter, of course I could." And now you have 2,000 words in tips.

You're on the way.

You've cracked the hardest bit by doing that.

What does 50 words look like?

"Remember when you're studying someone's face to look for the little red triangle in the corner the eye disappearing. The red triangle is called the caruncle, and when it disappears by the movement of the lower eyelid towards the nose and upwards, then the person is showing concern."

Brilliant. What a piece of knowledge to have! I don't think there's 1% of 1% of 1% of the world that knows that little bit of knowledge, and you now know it.

So, how about this?

How about if you wrote about a page for every tip? You'd have a book of 60-100 pages.

Your Free Book Writing Template

I've created for you a clear and easy-to-use 'book writing template' to capture your ideas

 **TO DOWNLOAD YOUR FREE COPY NOW - GO TO**
WWW.PETERTHOMSON.CLUB/
BOOK-WRITING-TEMPLATE

Chapter 4 -
Creating Your Book
How many pages should you write?

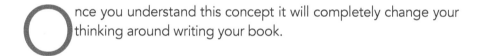

Once you understand this concept it will completely change your thinking around writing your book.

Here's the information...

I was told this by a man I rate so highly in the world. His name is Dan Sullivan.

He runs a business called Strategic Coach. He's been running that for about 25+ years.

He's been coaching for over 40 years, and as far as I'm concerned (for entrepreneurs who are very successful) he's the top man.

His information is amazing.

If you see any books by Dan Sullivan, go and buy them. They are brilliant.

He is a genius, as far as I am concerned.

So, what Dan says when it comes to writing a book...

Up to **60 pages**, the **readership** is **between 80% and 100%**.

Over 100 pages, readership **falls to 3%**.

Over 200 pages readership falls to under **1% of 1%**.

That means that only two or three people are reading it. You're reading it because you wrote it, and your relatives, they're reading it.

So, don't make the mistakes I have made over the years and write a book with 200 pages.

Write three books of 50-60 pages instead.

Not only...

Not only will you make more of an impact. Not only will you have more of an influence, but you'll also have more income, because a 60 – 80 page book sells for the same as a 200 page book.

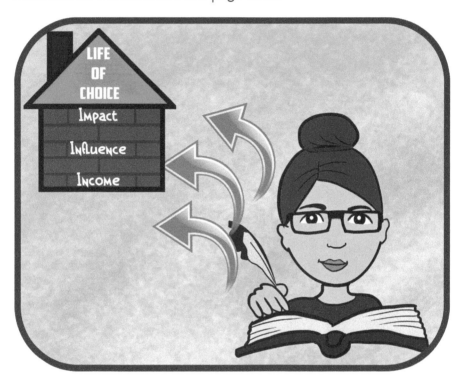

Here's an example:

I recently bought a book, called: 'Treat Your Own Neck' by Robin McKenzie. This book—which is 68 pages was £12.34 from Amazon.

Three of these books is £37, but he could produce them as just one book of about 200 pages and only get £12 for it.

Which would you prefer?

80% to 100% of people reading your stuff?

And receiving £36 for it rather than £12 for it? Take this idea to heart and you'll change more people's lives.

There's 400 words on a page in 10-point Verdana font. So, I'm going to show you how to write it...

I'm going to show you how much time it takes.

This the practical side of the creative side of being an author. Just like there is a practical side to all the famous artists... Take Da Vinci, for example.

I was in Milan recently and stood by *The Last Supper*. Da Vinci. It was painted by numbers. Everything was mapped out to the finest degree, including the number of the colours that he was using to create the Masterpiece.

That's what great artists do. We need to know the numbers, don't we? So, to complete your book you need 30 pages, each one having 400 words.

Most people could easily and fluently write at 25 words per minute. 25 words a minute is nothing.

This is what 25 words look like:

"Remember when you're studying someone's face to look for the little red triangle in the corner of the eye disappearing, it is called the caruncle."

Do you think you could type that in 1 minute?

I wrote it down and did the test; I can type at 72 words a minute. I've been writing for a long, long time, so maybe that's why. But I'm still going to use 25 words for our discussion.

So, if you have a page that's 400 words, and you can type at 25 words a minute, it takes just 16 minutes to write a page. (I think you'll do it even faster than 25 words a minute.)

So, to write 2 pages a day, it's going to take 32 minutes Let's say half an hour. Could you sit for ½ hour and write?

So, at the rate of 2 pages in a day, the writing of your book will be finished in 15 days. Let's space that out over 8 weeks. You need to write for ½ an hour a day for 2 days a week for 8 weeks. Yes?

Now, I have these important elements to add, and then I'm going to show you exactly how you do it even faster.

Within the book you want to add in things like quotes.

Here's a quote...

"If a person empties their purse into their head, no one can take it away from them - an investment in knowledge always pays the best interest"

- Benjamin Franklin

Here's another one...

"If your real desire is to be good, there is no need to wait for the money before you do it; you can do it now, this very moment, and just where you are."

-James Allen

Here's another one...

"If we wait for the moment when everything, absolutely everything is ready, we shall never begin..."

-Ivan Turgenev

You see, you are allowed to use quotes and put people's names on them. You could even take quite a chunk of stuff, as long as you credit it.

If the piece you're quoting, gets a little bit long, do what I do: go to the author of that work and ask their permission to use it.

I went to Professor Robert Cialdini, author of the brilliant book Influence Science and Practice and asked if it was OK if I use his material, 'Six Key Factors of Influence?' if I quoted the source and recommended the book. Of course, he said. "yes!"

Another book I read years ago, on negotiation, is called Everything is Negotiable (Great title!) by Gavin Kennedy. And I asked Gavin if I could quote a negotiation test from his book. He said, "yes!"

So, by all means, use a quote. Show the author's name. If you want to use more than, say, a quarter of a page, go to the person and ask their permission. I've never met anybody who's said no.

Include diagrams, graphs, action plans, pictures etc.

Now, here's a really important question...

What do you think is the first thing you write when you're writing your book?

Could it be the title?
Could it be the back page, the blurb all about you?

Let me tell you what you write first...

The first thing you write before you write any informational product is - the _order form_. On the order form, you write the benefits that the potential purchaser will experience.

Use this little expression...

"You're going to discover XXX, so you can..."

And clearly explain what the beneficial outcome will be for the person reading your book.

Chapter 5 -
Wine Glass & Smart Phone
Technique
~

This is where you can make a lot of money. Let me explain this for you.

Use / download a voice recording app on your phone

You sit down with a friend and a bottle of wine (or whatever you like to drink (even a glass of water), and you come up with a list or a MindMap of the ideas you're going to discuss about the subject you're passionate about. This is what you're going to turn into your tips booklet.

This is where we're going to start...

So, talk to a good friend using your notes. Talk for 2 hours and answer the questions they ask you about the notes you made.

You don't have to do it in one session.

Could you talk for 2 hours about the subjects you're passionate about? Of course, you could! At the end of 2 hours of talking, you will have about 16,000 words.

Then simply send the recording away. You can find plenty of online transcription services. (Otter.ai. Rev.com etc) Don't sit and do it yourself— no need to. And then you'll have your book transcribed.

Just edit the material yourself for your final product.

If you want to make an audio programme then you will talk for 6 hours.

Now, let me share this with you...

You create your tips booklet. One of mine is called "**117 Ways to Get Almost Anyone to Do Almost Anything.**" This sells for about £5 or $7, or thereabouts.

You take the same material and expand on the tips and create your softback version of the book, this sells for about £12.

Turn it into a hardback version, and it will sell for £20

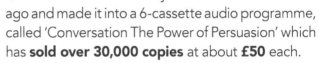

What's the difference between the softback version for £12 and the hardback version at £20?

The Secrets of Communication

Peter Thomson

Cardboard—that's the *only* difference.

The book example I used previously *'The Secrets of Communication'* I voiced years ago and made it into a 6-cassette audio programme, called 'Conversation The Power of Persuasion' which has **sold over 30,000 copies** at about **£50** each.

That's, **£1.5 million**.

A **video** series may be **£200**…

This is the way it works when you take your information and provide it in the way your audience wants to receive it—not the way you want to give it, but the way the audience wants to receive it. Then they can learn it, so they can use it, and so they can change their lives with it.

That's what you do.

You go from tips to book to audio to online to offline to maybe a mentoring programme…

I also have another product *'The Accelerated Business Growth System'*, which is 36 CDs & DVDs. It is available online, and it comes with 3 workbooks, printed on both sides.

So, that's 36 CDs & DVDs (72 discs at 20 minutes each) and sells for £3,000. We sold 600 of them, plus white-label versions. That's **£1.8 million**.

Tips booklet, book, audio, video, combined, mentoring…
Who knows where! One-on-one? It can be whatever you decide it to be.

 **TO DOWNLOAD YOUR FREE COPY NOW - GO TO**
WWW.PETERTHOMSON.CLUB/
BOOK-WRITING-TEMPLATE

Chapter 6 - Creating Your Avatar

At the start of the book, I mentioned the four questions:

- Who am I?
- Who are they?
- Who am I to them?
- Who are they to me?

We must have clarity about our customer avatar.

Let me tell you what the blank spaces are in the avatar diagram. What I urge you to do is to say to yourself, "Let's get clarity on my audience," and then fill in the questions to define who it is you're talking to.

1. **'Who?'** is the first one. *Who am I talking to?*
2. 'If I had a **magic wand** and I could share anything with them, **what would I share?'** (Thanks to Joanna Martin for this question)
3. What are their **fears**? What keeps people **awake at night?**
4. Next box up **'frustrations'**.
5. Then **'needs'** and **'wants'**.

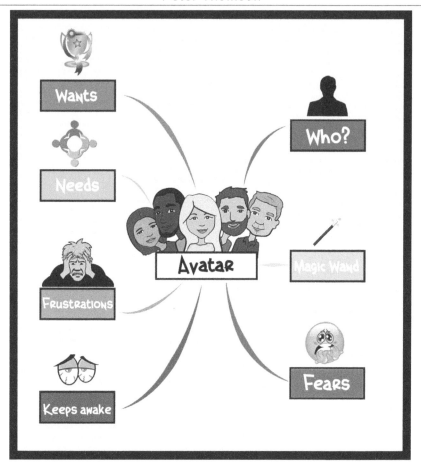

I'll give you some ideas based on my own client avatar...

- *Who am I talking to?*
- I'm talking to coaches, trainers, speakers, etc.

- *If I had a magic wand, what would I get for them?*
- Well, I'd get them more money and more respect.

- *What's their fears?*
- Here's a big one: **Insignificance!**

- *What keeps them awake?*
- Irregular income, rather than regular income.

- *What are their frustrations?*
- They are frustrated with having learned a lot they are not implementing or using effectively.

- *What do they need?*
- They need hand-holding—help from somebody who has travelled the road to help them achieve their goals.

- *What do they want?*
- They want significance. They want to make a difference. They want to be rightfully rewarded.

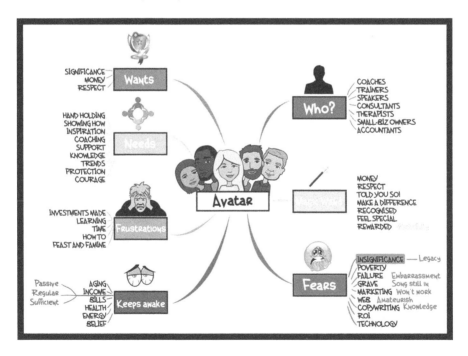

I urge you to do this exercise for yourself, because it gives you your demographics (who they are) and your psychographics (why they will buy).

41

Chapter 7 -
Creating Your Lead Magnet

'm going to show you how to create a lead magnet, or a *'golden carrot'* as we sometimes call it, or a freemium, premium, free report, free guide.

Clients of mine have been using *free information* as the top of their marketing funnel for about 20 years now. I've been using it for a little more than that.

Giving fabulous, quality information is the best way to go to market. Don't hide your good stuff. Get it out there and share it with people, because when they look at it, they say, "Wow!"

So, let's make a product for you that you can use for lead generation. So, what we're going to do is we're going to look at:

- Perspective
- Problem
- Pain
- Possible solution
- Pleasure
- Plan of action.

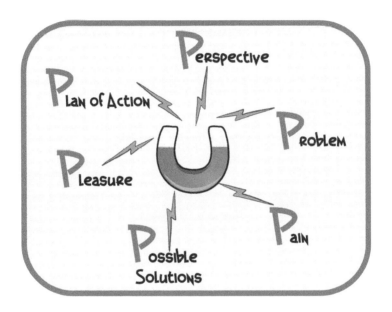

Imagine you were going to write a report...

When it's a **cold audience**, an audience that doesn't know you, you want to use an *away motivated title*.

Here's an example of an *away motivated headline* I've used...

"The 7 big mistakes business owners unwittingly make costing them a fortune in lost turnover, lost profits... And what's even worse lost personal cash... and how to avoid them.
Mistake #6 is costing people at least £25,000 a year."

Now, that's lots of words and it's so powerful. I've used it for years, and it just works brilliantly.

Here's an example of a *towards motivated headline*...

'Having Your Own Info Products to Reinforce Your Message Can Make You at Least 50,000 Every Year!'

Take it away. Don't copy. Use the idea as a template, create your own version.

To write the 'big mistakes'...

- You talk about the perspective.
- You talk about the problem that somebody has (this is for each of the mistakes).
- You talk about the pain the problem creates.
- You talk about possible solutions you can provide.
- You explain the exact solution.
- Then you explain the pleasure associated with that solution.
- Then you tell the reader what to do.

To write each of the tips/mistakes for your free report...

You clearly give some perspective to the idea you're about to cover.

Then you detail the first problem or mistake.

Then you explain the pain that problem causes to the reader.

Then you go through your suggested solution for the problem.

Then go into detail about the pleasure or benefits the reader will experience by doing what you're suggesting.

Then say precisely what they need to do to get the result you've outlined.

Do this for each of the problems/mistakes you're covering in your report.

Here's a brief example:

Let's say I wanted to write a free report on Time Management.

Here's how that would go:

Perspective:

As you and I know there's no such thing as – Time Management. Time just passes by. We can't control or manage it. We can only control and manage ourselves in and through time.

Problem:

The biggest problem faced by most people today – is the amount of time taken up, or perhaps better said as time spent – on emails, unnecessary emails.

Pain:

Just imagine – most people spend up to an hour a day on emails that do not need their attention or aren't worth the value of their time.

An hour a day equates to 5 hours per week, 2 days per month, 24 days per annum. A whole month wasted each year on unnecessary emails!

Potential Solution:

Restrict email time and block senders whose emails you do not need to see.

Pleasure:

Just imagine: 1 hour a day of extra useable time. If your time is worth 100 per hour then you can gain an extra £500 worth of time per week by saving one hour a day. That's £25,000 worth of time each year! £100,000 of time in just 4 years!

What will you do with all that valuable time?

Plan of Action:

Here are my suggestions:

1. Decide on 3 times per day you'll check your email.
2. I suggest 9:00 am, 12:30 and 4:30 pm.
3. Switch off any email notification.

Every time you receive an email decide if you wish to receive further emails from that person.

If you do – add them to your whitelist.
If you don't - block the email.
If the volume of emails is becoming a problem, check for those lists you can unsubscribe from or invest in a blocking program.

Enjoy the extra Time!

That's it!

The three magic words...

People talk to me, and they say, "Oh, writer's block.."

Rubbish! Get going! Get on with it! If you struggle ever with a blank screen in front of you, just start typing with one of these three words: 'of' or 'because' or 'and'

Let me give you an 'of' example...

"Of all the skills you and I could have, the one that stands head and shoulders above the others, is our ability to communicate our knowledge, experience and expertise."

You see, all I did was say 'of' and kept typing. That's all you do. You simply start talking with your fingers. So, don't be worried about writer's block.

"Because you're reading this now, there's one thing I know about you. You're interested in getting your knowledge and experience, and expertise to a greater number of people than you've ever done in the past, and you're looking for me to help you in some way to do that, or you wouldn't be sat here reading this now."

All I did there was start with 'because' and kept talking. This is all you must do. You wouldn't ever consider that you had speaking block, would you? No!

So ...

It's all about confidence. You must live in a little village just south of arrogant, not north of cocky, just south of arrogant.

Always include these:

Always include a promotion in your free report. (the webinar, the next event, the next book, the programme), web links, your telephone and your email (if you want to give it out), so people can contact you, and *always, always* have a call to action.

 TO DOWNLOAD YOUR FREE COPY NOW - GO TO
WWW.PETERTHOMSON.CLUB/
BOOK-WRITING-TEMPLATE

Chapter 8 - The 9 Step Lead Generation System

~

N ow I'm going to show you how to use your free report.

When creating your free report for a market that doesn't know you, make sure you use an **away motivated message**.

I've used this headline on so many websites and promotional pieces.

Attention: coaches, consultants, speakers, trainers, business owners...
"Not Having Your Own Information Products to Reinforce Your Message You Sacrifice At Least 50,000 Every Year!"
How much might you have lost already?'

So, now we're going to go through the lead generation process.

Announcement

When you go to the market, you're going to announce you have a free report available. That may be an announcement by email, maybe a Facebook post, a LinkedIn post.

1. Then you're going to provide the free report.

It's probably going to be a download, but it could be a physical tips booklet or a book.

2. Follow Up

A follow up call. (Not by you) if you are the person who provides the service, but by someone else.

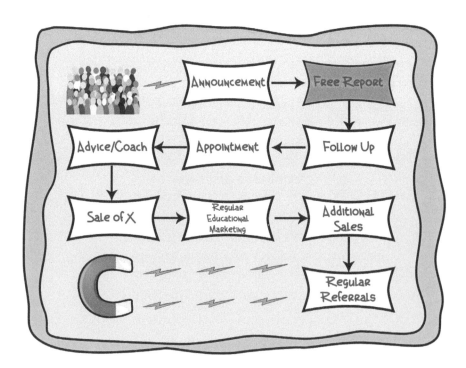

3. Appointment

During that follow up call an appointment is made for you. During that appointment (either face to face or on the phone or on Zoom), you're going to provide advice or coaching, provide value.

4. Sell Something

Then (if appropriate), you're going to sell something (i.e., the next step— the product or service you sell).

5. Regular Educational Marketing

And because that person who asked for the report is now a client or a customer, you're going to engage in regular educational marketing to keep in touch and continue to demonstrate your expertise.

6. Additional Sales

Then you're going to make additional sales, and then you're going to get regular referrals.

The critical mistake most people make on the follow up call:

Do you have any thoughts as to what it might be? (And sadly, most people make this mistake)

When I ask my audience this during a presentation, they say they'd ask:

- "Have you read the report?"
- "What was the best thing you liked about it?"
- "What did you take away?"

No! don't ask these questions.

The question you ask is...

'I don't suppose you've had a chance to read it yet, have you?'

That will usually prompt a 'no' answer, because most people who have downloaded your free report—however good it is—won't have read it.

They've downloaded it to their device. They've put it into their PDF reader. They put it on their phone or their iPad or whatever pad they use, and they still haven't read it. I know this is true from my experience over 25 years.

Most people will probably not have read stuff you've sent to them that they've asked for.

So, why would we ever dream of asking a question that assumes they have? *That's the wrong way around.*

Let's assume they haven't and ask the question appropriately. If the person says no, it's not a problem.

Respond by saying, "Well, no doubt you've been busy. Now, the reason that I wanted you to have the free report is this…" and on you go.

If they say, "Well actually, yes I have." then say, "Oh, great!" And continue anyway. It doesn't make any difference!

The purpose of having the free report is to get someone to put their hand up in the marketplace in response to the title of your report to say, "That's me. Let's have a conversation."

That's how I've generated most of my leads.

Chapter 9 -
The Magic Ingredient
~

N ow, let's have a look at you how you make substantial and serious money.

First, we're going to talk about **The Magic Ingredient.**

You're going to share with people your knowledge, your experience, and your expertise, but most people miss the magic ingredient… and that's **'your take on it.'**

That's what separates you from the marketplace. Make sure you tell people your bit of it, your opinion, your take, your spin. This is what is important. Don't miss that out.

This is what people pay for.

We've talked about it before…

You can find how to write a book online or go to somebody who will charge you £1,000 to learn what I taught you today, if you want to. Or you can come to me, and I'll teach you how to do that AND give you my take on it.

The Beauty of Continuity

So, let's get to the heart of it now. Let's look at the possibilities of having a newsletter.

I had *The Achiever's Edge*. It was on cassettes when I originally launched it. Then in CD format, and sometimes we would provide a transcript. (I made it available online later.) Now it's a monthly web meet – live!

So, let's write down the numbers...

I think this is going to spark your inspiration. I won't say motivation because you can't motivate other people. You may be able to inspire them, but motivation is an inside job (with outside consequences).

Let me explain the numbers...

The Achiever's Edge was £9.97 + £2.97 towards post and packaging... So, it was a £13 product (about $20) per month, and there are 12 months in a year. I ran it for 13 years and we had an average of 1,500 subscribers per month over the period.

When you multiply those four numbers together you get to **£3,042,000**.

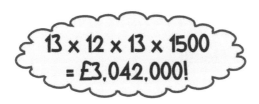

13 x 12 x 13 x 1500
= £3,042,000!

Most of my major clients came from The Achiever's Edge Subscriber base. So, I'm suggesting to you that once you put your knowledge into a tips booklet, and maybe you've turned it into a book, and maybe you've turned it into a training programme…

Maybe once you've turned it into a big programme of some description then take your knowledge and make a continuity product, a subscription product.

Let me tell you why…

In one of my mentoring groups was a woman who took away these ideas of a continuity product, and over a 5-year period she built an amazing platform of people that followed her, and now she has more than 6,000 subscribers on her subscription programme who pay her $30 a month.

6,000 x 30 is $180,000 per month!

Mark , another successful client and friend has a subscription product for online mentoring. It's the same idea of a continuity product, so I would urge you to create a continuity product of your own.

Let's have a look...

I'm going to go through the numbers for you...

Total Monthly Subscription rate.

Which is how much the subscription is and if you're physically sending it, how much P&P or shipping and handling you're adding to it.

What's the total of that? Let's say 20 for an example.

Subscribers Per Month

Averaging over a period - let's say 200.

I would think it would be reasonable with some time, effort, energy and focus and investment to get 200 subscribers if you took a year to get there.

When I went out with my first piece of marketing for The Achiever's Edge when it was the original cassette version, the first mailing brought me 1,151 subscribers.

I'm suggesting to you it takes a year to get 200. I think that number is reasonable.

Total Monthly Income

It would be 4,000 a month, based on this example.

Total Annual Income

Based on this example it would be 48,000 per year. Not a bad income for 200 subscribers!

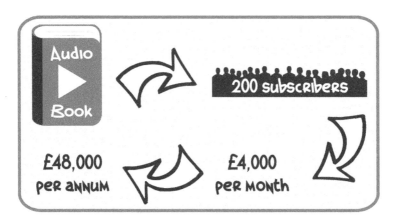

If you don't yet have a paid subscription product, I would urge you to do it. If you want to know more about how to do this perhaps you might decide to join me and *The Achievers Club* (I'll give you details at the end of this book)

I wonder what your income possibilities are?

Let's imagine for a moment that your income is at about 75,000 a year and you'd like to double that over some period to 150,000 per year with a split between fee income and product income.

I wonder now if maybe most of your income is fee based on swapping time for money, which I love doing as well, but it isn't the only thing I want to do in my life, because I like to have the other passive income.

If you wanted to have 40% fee income and 60% product sales income to get 150,000, you'd have to do 60,000 in fees and 90,000 in products.

What split do you want in the way of fees and products?

What timeframe would you like to do it in?

Let's talk about what you might have missed.

How many years have you been in business?

And then what about continuity income per annum?

Earlier we looked at a subscription product for continuity income, didn't we? 200 people generating about 50,000 a year.

So, if you've been in business for 10 years and you haven't had a subscription product for 10 years, you could have thrown away 500,000! If that's not inspirational, I don't know what is.

Chapter 10 -
Domino Marketing Method
~

The basis of the Domino Marketing Method is to offer amazing value right from the start of your relationship with a potential client.

'Fire your big guns first.' That's an expression by Herschell Gordon Lewis. In other words, go out into the marketplace, offer fabulous free information (your big guns) and then only ever sell the next action.

If you're sending an email to somebody you want to click through to a website, don't sell anything other than that click.

If you're on a website and you want someone to buy a product, just sell that click. If you're on the phone making an appointment, sell the appointment.

Now, where do we erect the pay wall? You erect the pay wall after you've provided ongoing quality information.

List Building

This is the system I use: my Simple Survey System. The easiest way to build a list is to go and ask people what they want.

You can go to LinkedIn, you can go to Facebook, you can go to whatever email list you have you can rent lists, you can go buy lists, you can go to other people's lists.

Go with a survey and add a bonus...

And the bonus could be your tips booklet, or it could be the first three chapters of your book, or it could be a prize draw. Ask people to give you information about what are their problems, their frustrations - what solutions they are looking for.

Then make your last question on your survey a yes/no question where you ask them to tick 'yes' or 'no' if they would like to have a conversation with you about a specific service or product you provide. This works so well!

Surveys are one of the best ways of building a list of people who've told you what it is they want from you.

Conclusion

I wish you every success in your journey to help other people by sharing your knowledge, experience, expertise (and your take on it).

If I can help you – please, do let me know.

Here's a short piece I wrote for the intro to a friend's book. It seems just so appropriate to the journey we're both on.

**There is a moment in every person's life
When the awareness of their destiny
Bursts like a bubble onto the surface of their conscious
mind It is at this moment that the weak avoid the
realisation and busy themselves with the mundane tasks
of their days
It is also at this moment that the strong awake and
decide to take action to change the world, their world, for
the better – and by so doing
secure for themselves their rightful and valued place in
the history of humankind**

Seize the moment to share what you know.

The world's been waiting for you.

Peter Thomson Bio

Peter Thomson is now regarded as the UK's leading strategist on business and personal growth. Starting in business in 1972 he built 3 successful companies – selling the last to a public company, after only 5 years trading, for £4.2M enabling him to retire at age 42.

Since that time Peter has concentrated on sharing his proven methods for business and personal success via audio and video programmes, books, seminars, conference speeches and mentoring programmes.

With over 100 audio and 100 video programmes written and recorded he is Nightingale Conant's leading UK author.

Peter specialises in helping coaches, consultants, speakers, trainers and small-business owners share more of their authentic messages with more people than they could ever reach on a 1-to-1 basis by showing them how to write and create and market their own informational products.

To talk to Peter email: sucess@peterthomson.com

Testimonials

Here are just 4 testimonials from previous clients I've worked with.

I was a member of Peter's membership programme and also had monthly 1 to 1 sessions at Peter's home (highly recommended!) Soon into the programme Peter helped me to focus on producing a video-based product as my strength is presenting and training. To cut a long story short, through Peter's invaluable, informal and fun mentoring I now have a video programme, the Limbic Performance System (LPS), which has changed my life. I no longer need to train unless I want to, and LPS made around £250,000 in just 1 year from its launch.

Estimated sales in the 12 months following are around £1,000,000.

Steve Neale - BCS International Ltd

"Working with Peter over a period of 18 months I created additional profits of over £100,000 using his ideas."

Mark Wickersham, Accountant

When Peter began his Mentoring Club we joined as founder members along with our eldest son and then our youngest son who wants to start his own business as a life coach. Since rejoining Peter we've written a marketing book for pharmacy contractors, which we would never have done without Peter's simple techniques, created our monthly membership with a deluxe version which is working very well AND have TWO £1,000,000 products.

So, we would recommend anybody who is serious about investing in themselves and their business to join with Peter. It is worth every penny.

Chris & Lynda Chanin

Since being part of Peter's group I can attribute at least £250,000 of income over the last 2 years from having the Book/DVD/CD pack

Rob Purfield